FINISHING LINE PRESS

www.finishinglinepress.com

# LANGUAGE LIKE WATER

*Poems*

# Nancy Gerber

*Finishing Line Press*
Georgetown, Kentucky

# LANGUAGE LIKE WATER

## ACKNOWLEDGMENTS

I would like to thank my writing friends who have supported and encouraged
me: Ellen Sherman, all these many years; Fran Bartkowski, for helpful
revisions; Lisa Sturm; Emily Blumenfeld; Patricia McKernon Runkle, and
Rosemary McGee.

I'd also like to thank the poets in the here-and-now and the hereafter who
have mentored and inspired me: Christine Redman-Waldeyer, Sondra Gash,
and Gail Fishman-Gerwin.

"Curvature" appeared in Adanna, Vol. 7, 2017.

Publisher: Leah Huete de Maines
Editor: Christen Kincaid
Cover Photograph: Otsego Lake, by Joshua Gerber. Used by permission.
Author Photo: Bob Gerber
Cover Design: Elizabeth Maines McCleavy

Order online: www.finishinglinepress.com
also available on amazon.com

Author inquiries and mail orders:
Finishing Line Press
PO Box 1626
Georgetown, Kentucky 40324
USA

# Contents

*In memory of my mother, Trudy Frankel (1928-2016)*

Before you know kindness as the deepest thing inside,
you must know sorrow as the other deepest thing.

—Naomi Shihab Nye,
"Kindness"

We are all carrying our mothers, and we are all better
daughters with the dead.

—Diannely Antigua,
"We Never Stop Talking About Our Mothers"

**Language Like Water**

This is how mothers and daughters speak,
language like water
without form or shape
a fluid holding of all things—
dreams, hopes, secrets.
Bodies.
Longings.

Fused,
floating
oceanic embrace

## Words as Swords

Trapped. The two of us,
poisoned by anger.
After all these years
I accuse our painful words.

Silence heals.
No words
for the time
before memory

before argument tore
us apart. A time
of wordless touch.

## Portrait of Mother and Daughter

Maybe I could paint us—
a pair of overlapping circles.
Spheres of blue and purple,
crimson red.
The colors of women,
bruised and bleeding.
Not beautiful.
True nonetheless.

## The Night I Tripped, Age Three

The night I tripped
on the cord

of the humidifier,
on my way

to the toilet,
a glass sphere

of scalding water
near my bed,

I remember screaming
as my skin sizzled.

I must have fainted.

I woke in a doctor's
office, blinding light

prone, leg wrapped
in bandages

like a mummy.
My mother

weeping at the
foot of the table.

Yes, the doctor
nodded. Bed rest.

Then she'll be
ok.

Consolation: a stuffed
Steiff tiger puppet,

cost my dad
a fortune.

Near my knee still a scar,
puckered souvenir

that burning night.

## Ballet Class

Plump girl, pink tights
facing the mirrored wall
at Miss Sue's.

I'm not like the others,
blond hair, smug
lips, twiggy legs.

My hair is short, dark.
I don't smile.
Something is wrong

with my mother.
She locks herself
in the bedroom

I hear her sobs
through the door.

I don't like Miss Sue's
way. I prefer
my own. This

angers Miss Sue.
She tells my mother
I'm immature

while others listen
with rapt attention.
"She's four!"

my mother explodes.
She grabs my hand.
Together we run

down the stairs.
My mother's face
is moist. I want

to touch her cheek.
I want to ask if I'm
the reason she's so sad

## Barbie

I wanted a Barbie.
You told me no.

Instead Tammy,
legs thick as tree trunks

a ring of frizzy hair—
just like mine,

not a bombshell.
Barbie had long

lovely tresses,
curvaceous breasts,

went steady with Ken.
Tammy had no one.

I dreamed of Barbie's
svelte legs, floral

bikinis, nights
on the town.

Finally you gave in.
A Barbie! But never Ken.

## My Mother's Voice

Unhappiness tailed my mother like a comet,
kept her locked in her room school afternoons.
I'd open the front door, sit in the kitchen,
a bag of Chips Ahoy for company.
In the house my mother's silent cries.

Years later as we drove past her school
she burst into song, the football cheer:
"Lower Merion, Lower Merion,
Fill your lungs and sing!"
My mother's voice, full and rising,
uplifted by something I did not know
and could not name.

## The Closet

That day in your bedroom
after I lost all that weight
you flung open the closet. Grabbed slacks
and blouses from hangers,
threw them at me.

"Here, take this! And this!"
Clothes dropped to the floor,
funereal, abandoned.

"I don't want them," I said.

You were enraged, proof
we were not the same.
"These are clothes for a woman
your age,
not mine."
I tried to explain.
But the avalanche kept coming,

pushing me farther away.

## The Color of Madness

Your face a buttercup,
a singular yellow,
a sheet of wax
pressed thin.

Thunderclouds exploded
inside you, squalls of terror
bursting
till you capsized.

From the kitchen window
parched tufts
of dandelions
dotted our lawn.

At the house next door,
small rocks circled
the towering spruce.
That's what I saw.

Did you see shadowy beasts
roaming the jungle?
Did they echo the voices
roaring inside you?

## My Mother's Wisdom

In the armchair framed
by sunlight, she told me
"Letting go
            is the hardest part."
We were chatting,
not our habit.
The subject, my children.
But she could have meant more:
her grip on memory,
her connection to me.
Meaning didn't matter.
Those words—
the hard shell of us
finally
            cracked open.

## Queen of Bakeries

My mother was known
as the Queen of Bakeries,
traveling twenty miles
or more, for cakes, pastries.

Suffern for rugelach
Teaneck for babka,
Nyack for linzertorte
Englewood for lemon bars.

The January she turned eighty,
last birthday before dementia
wrecked her mind
she bought three cakes

to take to the restaurant.
Displayed on the kitchen table—
frosted carrot, coconut,
chocolate mousse.

*I'm bringing all three.*

You can't, I say.
Too many.
One cake, that's all.
Her eyes filled with tears.

I was cruel to make her choose.

## A Good Daughter

If I were good
I wouldn't have put you
in a nursing home.

I would have cared
for you
as you cared for me.

Changed you, fed you,
rocked you when
you wept.

Instead I let
strangers feed you,
change you—

they never held you.
When I came
to visit
you never spoke

and though
you never spoke
to anyone

your silence,
an accusation.

A good daughter
doesn't put her mother

in a place like this.

## Curvature

My mother lies curved
like a seahorse
Bones poking through
bruised
jellyfish skin
Coiled in her shell,
mind out of reach.

I whisper
to her clam-shut eyes
"I am here."
I place my finger
on her thin
blanched wrist.

## Today

I bought a book
for my dead mother

who loved solid weight,
creamy pages

inked in black,
covers like fine

art. The book
I bought

was by a woman
my mother read

just before
her memory

failed forever.
The book

she'll never open
is dressed in black

splashed with
golden poppies.

She loved all
blooming things.

## My Mother's Perfume

L'Air du Temps,
my mother's scent.
Floral, not too dear—
like Ricci, my mother
grew up poor.

At the drugstore
on glass shelves
the butter-yellow box,
ribbed flacon
crowned by a pair
of frosted doves
eternally embracing.
Love and peace,

the doves' song
in notes of peach
and rose,
enchantment for
my mother,
with her life
of disappointment.

## My Mother's Kugel

Whip fresh eggs, broad noodles,
sugar, sour cream,
orange juice, raisins.
Bake till golden crested.

My mother's kugel.
We shared it
Sunday mornings
just the two of us

luscious layers
bridging the distance,
fault lines dividing us,
a slice of peace.

## My Mother, a Rose

My mother
a white rose,
all color
stripped away.

My mother,
a dying rose.
One day she will
bloom again.

## Vintage

I thought I'd
never forgive.

*You'll see,* he said
when she passed.

*Fond recollections
will flood back.*

None for seven years.
Suddenly

There they were—
vintage rings

she found for
me at antiques

fairs, flea
markets. And I

could choose.
So many choices—

opal, ruby, pearl.
Their gold bands

enchanting,
circlets of truth—

my choice,
her love.

## A Stroll in the Park

Today I saw
myself walking with my mother—
the ghost
of my mother.

We strolled through a park,
the New England town
where I've lived
since Covid.

My mother would have
loved this place, its deep
rooted history, village green
flanked
by the towering church
dressed in white, the
slender spire

touching pale blue sky.

We're walking arm
in arm, which we never
did while she was alive.

We kept each other
arm's length—her silence,
my anger or was it
the other way
round

Today we're quiet.
She would have
loved this peace.

**Nancy Gerber** is the author of two poetry chapbooks, *The Kingdom of Childhood* and *We Are All Refugees,* published by New Feral Press. She is the author of seven full-length books —a scholarly monograph, as well as memoir and fiction. Her book of short stories, *A Way Out of Nowhere,* was awarded the Independent Press Award; *Fire and Ice: Poetry and Prose* was a finalist for the Gradiva Award from the National Association for the Advancement of Psychoanalysis. She received a PhD in English from Rutgers University and completed psychoanalytic training at the Academy of Clinical and Applied Psychoanalysis in Livingston, New Jersey, where she is a member of the faculty. She resides in Connecticut.